Coatbridge
Then & Now

Sandra Malcolm

The North British Railway had a number of stations in and around Coatbridge: this one was named Coatbridge and opened in 1842. It was renamed Coatbridge Central in 1953 after the 1826-built Monkland and Kirkintilloch Railway station, called Coatbridge Central, closed; its entrance was at the corner of Main Street and Sunnyside Road. The Monkland and Kirkintilloch Railway was built to transport coal to the Forth and Clyde Canal.

Text © Sandra Malcolm, 2020.
First published in the United Kingdom, 2020,
by Stenlake Publishing Ltd.,
54-58 Mill Square,
Catrine, Ayrshire,
KA5 6RD

Telephone: 01290 551122
www.stenlake.co.uk

Printed by P2D,
1 Newlands Road,
Westoning,
MK45 5LD

ISBN 9781840338492

**The publishers regret that they cannot supply
copies of any pictures featured in this book.**

Acknowledgements

The author would like to thank the staff of Summerlee Heritage Museum, in particular David Craig. This book is dedicated to the McKeowns and Devlins of Coatbridge.

Further Reading

The books and websites listed below were used by the author during her research. Only *Old Coatbridge Villages* is available from Stenlake Publishing. Those interested in finding out more are advised to contact their local bookshop or reference library.

Peter Drummond and James Smith, *Coatbridge: Three Centuries of Change*, Lanarkshire Family History Society, 2004.
Oliver van Helden, *Old Coatbridge Villages*, Stenlake Publishing, 1997.
www.monklands.co.uk
www.railscot.co.uk

Introduction

A crannog in Lochend Loch (or, as it is known locally, Drumpellier Loch) is the earliest evidence of human habitation in the Coatbridge area. On the piece of land between Drumpellier and Bargeddie a Bronze Age cemetery has been found and there is evidence of Roman occupation. The main Celtic tribes in the area during Roman times were the Damnonii and Selgovae.

The Monklands area got its name from the monks of Newbattle Abbey, who were granted the lands in 1162, a time when some of the Caledonian Forest was still evident in the area. It was the monks who were the first to mine coal in the area and they also began extensive cultivation of the lands. In the fifteenth century 'black stones' were distributed as alms to the poor and in the sixteenth century the first references to 'black gold' were recorded. By that time most of their lands had been leased to farmers.

In 1602 Sir Thomas Hamilton of Binning bought the lands, with the Clelands of Monklands taking possession in 1633. In 1639 James, Marquis of Hamilton, was the owner and later the land was owned by the College of Glasgow. In 1641 the parish of Monklands was divided between New Monkland (now Airdrie) and Old Monkland (now Coatbridge).

In 1770 an Act of Parliament was passed to allow work to start on the Monkland Canal. The canal provided a perfect link with Glasgow and ultimately the coal, iron and fireclay industries, which developed as a result, changed the landscape forever. The main reason for the existence of the canal was clearly stated at the outset: it would 'reduce the price of coal, to be of advantage to the manufacturers of Glasgow'. In 1793 four collieries were opened along the banks of the canal, with over 400 men employed in each colliery. The amount of work available fuelled a surge in the population. In 1755 the number of people living in Old Monkland was 1,813; by 1831 it was 9,580.

In the early part of the nineteenth century, two events happened which further industrialised the area: the discovery of a large seam of blackband ironstone and J.B. Neilson's discovery that preheating air before passing it through blast furnaces made the iron smelting process considerably more efficient. Once again, the industrialists immediately expanded their businesses by increasing the capacity at Calder and Gartsherrie and building new iron works at Dundyvan, Calderbank, Summerlee, Carnbroe and Langloan.

In the early 1830s the town of Coatbridge was given a formal standing when the Baird family (who owned Gartsherrie Iron Works) laid out the main streets and some buildings. Even by 1840 the Coatbridge area was described as 'one large village', but over time the modern town was formed by the amalgamation of a number of villages: Old Monkland and Kirkshaws, Coatbridge, Coatdyke, Dundyvan, Gartsherrie, Langloan and Whifflet.

The coming of the railways further increased industrialisation of the area. In 1826 the Monkland and Kirkintilloch Railway opened, and later the Ballochney and the Wishaw and Coltness railways. The Garnkirk and Glasgow Railway opened in 1831. It competed directly with the canal as it ran directly alongside it.

By 1840 Scotland had 88 furnaces for the manufacture of iron, 65 of which were in the Coatbridge area. However, the intensity of the industry could not last forever and by 1864 the supplies of blackband ironstone were almost exhausted. The environmental impact on the area was devastating. In the 1885 *Ordnance Gazetteer of Scotland* the landscape was described thus: 'Fire, smoke, and soot, with the roar and rattle of machinery, are its leading characteristics ….' It was not until 1885 that Coatbridge became a burgh and until that time there were no controls over working conditions, overcrowding or pollution control. Even when it became a burgh, the ironmasters were able to include clauses in the burgh bill to allow the blast furnaces to continue polluting the area.

By the end of the First World War there were only a few iron works left. Langloan closed in 1919, Calder and Carnbroe in 1921, and Summerlee in 1929. Gartsherrie was the last to close in 1967.

The effects of the industrial revolution on Coatbridge are still felt today. The areas of the present car parks on both sides of the South Circular Road are so undermined that no buildings of any great size can be built on them. Tenement height is restricted in some areas because of mine workings below. However, Coatbridge is currently undergoing regeneration schemes to improve the local area and Urban Aid, European Union grants and Social Inclusion Partnerships have all been part of efforts to restore the town.

Local tradition says that the original Old Monkland Parish Church was built at this spot by a pilgrim who had been told to carry a stone from Glasgow as penance and to build a church when he could go on no longer. Whatever the truth of its origins, land for the church was granted in 1170 by the monks of Newbattle Abbey and the present building, standing on Woodside Street, was erected in 1790, designed to seat 902. In 1780 the Rev. John Bower, then minister of the church, described Old Monkland as an immense garden with its fields, orchards and rivers abounding with salmon and trout. The church

hall was built around 1950. The cottages on the right were named Kirkstyle Cottages due to their proximity to the church gate. They were originally built for Douglas Estate workers and included a mission hall and a house for a missionary. Later demolished, a fruit and vegetable merchant was based on their site but more recently an indoor golf driving range has been set up. A more modern row of cottages (also called Kirkstyle) was erected in 1902 a little down the street from the driving range.

Old Monkland Public School

Old Monkland Public School was probably built soon after the passing of the 1872 Education Act and stood on the north corner of Woodside Street and Old Monkland Road. Prior to 1872, three private schools and four sessional schools had been under the supervision of the Kirk Session of Old Monkland Church. After the 1872 Education Act, Old Monkland Parish School Board took over the running of these schools. In the 1890s the head teacher of Old

Monklands School, Mr Lawrence, asked the board to provide the school with fuel and light, but the board 'resolved to adhere to their former determination on the matter', i.e. the request was denied! The building was still in existence in the 1960s though the houses seen in the photograph above were built later that decade. Houses built opposite mean that it is impossible to replicate the angle of the original photograph.

CANAL AT WEST END PARK, COATBRIDGE.   B.6074.

West End Park was formerly a local amenity tip, but was laid out as a park by a local benefactor, Sir John Wilson, in 1908. The chimneys in the background belong to the Langloan Iron and Chemical Works which operated between 1841 and 1919. The Janet Hamilton Memorial Fountain at the Bank Street side of the park is dedicated to the renowned Scottish poet who lived adjacent to the park in the Langloan Estate. Hamilton was born in Shotts in 1795, but moved to Langloan when she was seven, remaining until her death in 1873. Although her mother taught her to read at the age of five, she was 54 before she took up writing seriously. This may well have been because she had ten children to look after! She began writing for a magazine called *Working Man's Friend*. In

1866 she became blind, by which time she had become a widely respected poet. The main themes of her writing were social problems that affected the community and her work empathised with the oppressed. She is buried in Old Monkland Cemetery and on her headstone are the words 'she being dead yet speaketh'. The Monkland Canal, which can be seen in the foreground of the photograph on page 8, was essential to the area until the late 1860s, after which traffic began to decline. By the 1930s it had almost stopped and in 1952 an Act of Parliament extinguished rights of navigation. From that time it was considered that the derelict canal hindered proper re-planning of Coatbridge and over half the original canal and branches were either piped or infilled.

New St Andrew's Parish Church facing down Baird Street. Opened in 1839 as Gartsherrie Church, it was built for the benefit of workers, and their families, employed by William Baird & Co. Ironmasters. The architects of the building were Scott, Stephen and Gale of Glasgow and in 1870 a Willis organ was installed. The stained glass in the vestibule was designed by Alfred Webster who was considered 'one of the most accomplished younger Scots artists in stained glass' and designed windows for many churches all over Scotland. He was commissioned as a 2nd Lieutenant in the Gordon Highlanders in March 1915 and went to the front lines in the Ypres Salient in June. Two months later he was wounded while on patrol and died in hospital at Etaples on the 24 August 1915. The congregation today is an amalgamation of those from Dunbeath, Maxwell and Clifton churches.

Baird & Co. was at one time the largest manufactures of pig iron in Scotland. It began in 1816 when it leased the coalfield at Rochsolloch. Its first furnace at Gartsherrie was erected in 1828. The company was nationalised between 1946 and 1951 and the engineering side closed in 1967. It has since diversified into clothing, its brands including Lowe Alpine, Windsmoor, Danimac, Melka and Tennison. Behind the wall on the right of the old photo there was a school which incorporated Gartsherrie Academy, which had been opened by Baird & Co., in 1845. In 1908 the building became Coatbridge Public School and later Gartsherrie Academy Primary School. It closed in 1989 and lay derelict for some years before conversion into flats.

Sunnyside Road contained many shops, a shoe factory, a potato crisp factory, several pubs and many houses. This view was taken around the location of No. 64. In that area there was a coach house with stables and also a smiddy, a funeral office, a tea room, a draper's and a butcher's. Further down the street were two shops owned by the Salvation Army. The local Co-operative Society, founded in 1872, had a branch at No. 68.

In the middle of the old photograph on the previous page, further down Sunnyside Road can just be glimpsed the Lamberton building, which was built around 1879 for Baird & Co. who needed an engineering company to manufacture their Gartsherrie Coal Cutter, the first successful Scottish machine of this type. The building was acquired in 1882 by Lamberton & Co. engineers, who made heavy machinery for iron and steel industries. Lamberton's owned most of the original houses on Sunnyside Road, almost all of which no longer stand.

The Royal Hotel on the left of this photograph was originally the Coatbridge Inn, built by the Baird family in 1835. The North British railway station was just across the road. During the cholera epidemic of 1848 doctors held daily meetings here to assess the progress of the disease and try to find possible solutions to halting it (this epidemic began in Edinburgh and spread to Glasgow; the city's corporation built the water supply from Loch Katrine as a result). Airdrie tram No. 8 can also be seen, heading away from the Langloan Terminus along Main Street. During the First World War, Airdrie and

Coatbridge Tramways employed women to replace male staff serving in the armed forces. Initially, they were only hired as conductresses, but later on as motorwomen too. The tramway company had been formed by British Electric Traction to run the single line between the two towns. The Airdrie Savings Bank building is on the left (see page 21).

This fountain – seen in its present position in the previous photograph – is dedicated to Alexander Whitelaw, an industrialist and partner in Gartsherrie Iron Works. In 1872 he organised the relocation of the railway line away from the main street to a level above the canal in an effort to create a civic space. The original location of the fountain, seen here, was in front of the Royal Hotel (now the Airdrie Savings Bank building) at the point of the removed level crossing. It had been moved by 1933 because of increasing incidents of traffic congestion. The inscription on the fountain reads: 'This fountain stands on

the site of the level crossing of the Monkland and Kirkintilloch Railway which was removed in 1872. The fountain was inaugurated on 10 August 1875.' When fully working, it had constantly flowing clean drinking water for the general public with metal drinking cups on chains attached to each basin. It was moved again to the right corner of Main Street and the basins were filled in. The NBR Central Station, which opened in 1871 and closed in 1931, can be seen to the left of the fountain.

The junction to the right of and just beyond the van is Academy Street where it meets No. 30 Main Street. The bank buildings at the corner on the junction are still there today. They were built by the Clydesdale Bank although it no longer runs a branch from them. Further up Academy Street, though not in view here, is the old Carnegie Library which Andrew Carnegie himself officially opened on 7 June 1906. He received the ceremonial freedom of the Burgh of Coatbridge from Provost McCosh during the opening. The library cost £15,000 to construct. The premises closed in 2012 and the building has been

converted into flats. The large eagle above the doorway to the right belonged to the Eagle Inn at No. 55 Main Street, run by a widow, Mary Ann Flannigan. The annual rent in 1882 was £100 per annum. The junction with Church Street is on the right hand side, just at the shops' canopies. Many of the buildings seen here were demolished after the Second World War and replaced in the 1970s by modern concrete buildings. The street was regenerated in 2015.

MAIN STREET, COATBRIDGE

In the middle of the row of tenements seen here is Coia's Central Café at Nos. 27–29 Main Street, set within a narrow four-storey and basement 'Glasgow Style' former café, shop and domestic building. Built around 1926 by the architect Thomas Smith, the owner of the building was Charles Coia. In the basement was a billiards saloon and there was a shop and dance hall on the ground floor, and a restaurant on the first floor with domestic flats above. By 1994 the building was vacant and in a deteriorating condition. It was owned in 1997 by the Charles Coia Trust, although subject to a dispute over

ownership within the Coia family. In 2012 planning permission was given for a nightclub in the basement and a bar and lounge with a function suite on the first floor although these are yet to materialise. Built in 1920 and opening for business in 1921, the tall domed building at the far left is the local branch of the Airdrie Savings Bank, which was instituted in 1853 with a board of directors comprising local tradesmen including a blacksmith, a weaver, a tailor, a stonemason and a salesman. The bank ceased business in 2017 and the branch now lies empty.

St Patrick's RC Church at No. 1 St John Street was founded in 1845 when Father William Walsh was appointed the first pastor to a new mission in Coatbridge. He celebrated Mass in a carpenter's shed in East Canal Street (now South Circular Road) and during the week the shed acted as a school. In 1847 he made plans for a new church on a site made available on St John Street by Messrs Baird & Co. at a nominal charge of one groat. Sadly, before the plans could materialise, Father Welsh died of typhus fever, aged 28. The church was built in 1848 by Welsh's successor, Father Michael O'Keeffe, who

stayed for 46 years. In 1866 the church was renovated and enlarged, but by this time it was evident that a new church would have to be built. On Sunday, 19 August 1894, the original church closed and demolition started the following day. On 17 May 1896 the new church, seen here, opened at a cost of £6,770-8-8*d*. Over the years there were further additions and renovations, the most recent of which was the installation of the Willis organ from Clifton Church in 2009.

MAIN STREET, LOOKING WEST, AND ST. PATRICK'S R.C. CHURCH, COATBRIDGE

In 1900 St Patrick's opened a new church hall to its side at a cost of £1,900. It contained a billiard hall and in 1925 it also had 88 card tables and 100 packs of cards; whist drives were very popular social occasions. The lorry is delivering soft drinks from the Barr Company. Robert Barr set up the business in

Falkirk in 1875, with a Glasgow business opening in 1887 under the management of his son. At the time Barr's was just one of hundreds of soft drinks companies in the country.

The Empire Theatre at Nos. 136–138 Main Street opened in October 1912 and presented variety shows. It became a cinema in 1920 when it was bought by George Singleton. He sold it in September 1936 to the Odeon group and after it was remodelled it became known as the Odeon. It closed in 1976 and was demolished to make way for shops. The local branch of the Buttercup Dairy (there were 250 across Scotland at one time) can be seen across the road

and the Employment Exchange is just beyond the theatre. The Clifton Iron Works can be seen in the centre of the picture. At No. 128 Main Street, just beside the Theatre was the Caledonian Tube Works, established in 1844 for the manufacture of lap welded iron tubes for steam boilers. This was taken over by the Scottish Tube Co., which in turn was taken over by Stewarts & Lloyds in 1931. It closed in the 1960s.

With the parish of Gartsherrie Church, Coats Church was opened at the corner of Muiryhall Street and Jackson Street in 1875 due to the increase in the local population. Around 1977 the church was damaged by fire and partly rebuilt afterwards. It changed its name to Clifton Parish Church in 1993 following a union of the Coatdykes and Coats congregations. The church closed in 2008 when Clifton and St Andrews congregations united to form New St Andrews Parish Church. The school to the right was St Patrick's RC on Jackson Street, now St Andrew's High. It was founded in 1845 by Father William

Walsh as St Patrick's Mission in St John Street. The new building was opened in 1905 at a cost of £5,406. Two former pupils of the school, Dr John Reid and Helen Liddell (Baroness Liddell of Coatdyke), served in Tony Blair's cabinet. A new St Patrick's RC opened in Old Monkland Road in 2006 after an amalgamation with Columba High. The site seen here is now occupied by Coatbridge High School which amalgamated with Rosehall High in 2008.

Seating 2,000, the Theatre Royal opened at No. 181 Main Street in 1875. In the same year it was used as a venue for the grand evening banquet following the unveiling and inauguration of the Whitelaw Memorial Fountain. In October 1890 part of the gallery collapsed because of dry rot, though no one was badly hurt. It transpired that all the wooden supports in the theatre were infected and all had to be replaced with iron girders. It was sold to R.C. Buchanan in January 1907, during which year a young Charlie Chaplin appeared as part of Fred Karno's Mumming Brothers act. The first film was shown

in the theatre on 19 April 1915 and after that it was used as a cinema and variety show venue. W. Regent bought it in 1938 and it then became a full-time cinema. It was sold to Green's in 1956, by which time its capacity was 460 in the stalls and 206 in the balcony. The locals called the gallery the 'hen's roost'. The building closed on 9 August 1958 and lay derelict until it was demolished for road widening in 1966. The Odeon further down the street was later demolished (see page 26).

At malleable iron works pig iron was melted in puddling furnaces which turned it into a purer form of iron known as 'wrought' iron. On removal from the furnace it was hammered, whilst still hot and soft, into the shapes of countless products. The Phoenix Iron Works was erected in 1861 and by 1864 had six puddling and two heating furnaces, with engines and machinery capable of producing 250 tons of finished iron in a month. By the time of closure in 1921, the works had 38 puddling furnaces. The Clifton Iron Works also opened in 1861, adjacent to the Phoenix works and built by Messrs Colville and Gray at a cost of £7,000. Manufacture began in February 1862. These works could produce 600 tons of finished malleable iron per month and closed in

1913. Both works stood at the foot of Jackson Street and caused immense pollution over the area around Main Street and nearby workers' tenements. They were amalgamated into the Scottish Iron & Steel Co. Ltd. which changed its name to Bairds & Scottish Steel Ltd in 1938. This was nationalised in 1951 when it became known as the Iron and Steel Corporation of Great Britain. On denationalisation in 1963 the company changed its name to Iron and Steel Investments, but by 1967 it was no longer viable and was closed.

Once Coatbridge Tram Depot on Main Street, this building is now used as a kitchen showroom. The depot opened in 1904 and closed in 1956. Afterwards, it became Watson's garage, the area's main Vauxhall dealer. Between 1904 and 1922 Airdrie and Coatbridge Tramways (owned by British Electric Traction,

a large British industrial conglomerate) operated a tramway service. It was taken over by Airdrie and Coatbridge Corporations in 1920 for the sum of £77,550 and the line was extended to Baillieston. In 1922 the line was acquired by Glasgow Corporation Tramways for £82,250.

The Old Toll Bar at the corner of East Muiryhall Street and Main Street occupied the site where the toll house stood up until around 1885. The toll bar was on the turnpike road from Coatbridge to Glasgow which opened in 1795. When the toll house was demolished a new building was erected and David

Couper obtained the license. His public house had rooms that were richly upholstered and had beautiful mirrors decorating the walls. He owned a number of other public houses in the area and all were fitted out to the same high standard.

When A.J. Stewart relocated his iron founding business from Glasgow in the 1860s, Coatdyke changed from a small village into a busy, polluted area. Airdrie had obtained burgh status in 1821 and that brought with it some rules and regulations with regard to pollution. Coatbridge had no such status

until 1885 and it was probably the lack of regulations that brought A.J. Stewart into the area. The tenement was built in 1896. The recruiting poster on the delivery cart was created in 1915 by the Parliamentary Recruiting Committee. Strangely, it was mainly used in Australia.

Residents of Rochsolloch Road had a direct view of the iron works of the same name. The pollution from them led to the area having a notorious reputation for being an unhealthy place to live and work.

Life expectancy for men was 49 years and for women it was 52 years. Nowadays, life expectancy in this area is 75 years for men and 80 years for women. These houses (previous page) were still standing in the 1960s but were demolished the following decade.

In the centre of this photograph, at the top of Kippen Street, can be seen Rochsolloch Primary School which opened in 1902 and remained in use until 2017 when it moved to a joint campus with Alexandra Primary on Bellsyke Road. It is now called All Saint's Primary. Nothing remains of the old houses in Kippen Street. After the end of the Second World War all the old buildings were demolished as the housing was considered unfit for purpose. Stories

are told of outside toilets where a stick had to be kept to break the ice in winter. At the time of demolition around the 1950s, Laughlan's shop on the left had become Joe Beckett's greengrocer's.

Rochsolloch Iron Works opened in 1858. It had six puddling and two heating furnaces and was capable of producing nearly 200 tons of finished malleable iron in a month. The site had the advantage of being close to the Monkland Canal and the railway. In 1881 Rochsolloch works was incorporated into Waverley Iron and Steel Works and in 1912 the company amalgamated into the Scottish Iron & Steel Co. Ltd, a conglomeration of thirteen companies,

whose offices were based in Bothwell Street, Glasgow. The works closed in 1967, along with Gartsherrie, by which time it had 25 puddling furnaces. The buildings were known as 'the workie'; the land has since become the site of an industrial estate and a branch of an outdoor clothing retailer.

A.B. Donaldson was a grocer and confectioner at the corner of Calder Street and Garturk Street. In the window is an advert for Melrose Tea, a company founded by Andrew Melrose in 1812.

Following the collapse of the East India Company's monopoly in 1833, Melrose was the first merchant to land tea in Britain outside of London: the tea clipper *Isabella* carried the shipment into Edinburgh in 1835, an historic moment in the trading of tea.

In 1861 Old Monkland Church erected a parish poorhouse, designed by Robert Baird, at the south of what is now School Street and a large block was added in 1874. In 1865 the management of the poorhouse was severely criticised by the Board of Supervision after the death of a five year old boy, Thomas Cumnock, due to lack of proper care. Coathill Fever Hospital was erected on an adjoining site to the south east of the poorhouse (which is on the left of this view), though they were separate entities. In the 1930s and 1940s the poorhouse was operating as the Old Monkland Home Poor Law Institution. A 1946 report described its location as 'a depressing site in Coatbridge' with a 69-bed hospital and an asylum for 'milder types of lunatic'. The report described the interior – '… the main block of this institution is old and done, with dark corridors and crowded dormitories, and the impression is one of general neglect. The dining room is very gloomy.' – and recommended that the premises be abandoned. There is now a day hospital on the site, built in 2007, which provides a number of outpatient clinic services.